Le Cid

Crofts Classics

GENERAL EDITOR
Samuel H. Beer, *Harvard University*

PIERRE CORNEILLE

Le Cid

TRANSLATED AND EDITED BY
John C. Lapp
STANFORD UNIVERSITY

Harlan Davidson, Inc.
Wheeling, Illinois 60090-6000

Visit us on the World Wide Web at www.harlandavidson.com.

Library of Congress Cataloging-in-Publication Data

Corneille, Pierre, 1606–1684.
        Le Cid.

        (Crofts classics)
        Reprint. Originally published: New York: Appleton-Century-
        Crofts, 1955.
        Bibiliography: p. 00
        1. Cid., ca. 1043–1099 — Drama. I. Lapp, John C., 1917–.
        II. Title.
PQ1749.E5L3   1986   842'.4   86-8924
ISBN 0-88295-026-6 (pbk.)
ISBN 978-0-88295-026-6 (pbk.)

Manufactured in the United States of America
09 08 07 16 17 18 VP

INTRODUCTION

WHEN *Le Cid* was first performed in Paris, late in 1636 or in the early months of 1637, Pierre Corneille was already an established playwright although none of his nine previous works had met with outstanding success. Of these, all but one were comedies, closer in style and tone to Shakespeare's romantic comedies than to those of his great contemporary, Molière. The one tragedy, *Médée,* closely modelled after Seneca's version, was not a success, perhaps because Corneille's need to hew closely to the well-known plot frustrated his usual exuberance of invention. *Le Cid,* however, was a tremendous popular hit, combining all the elements calculated to please its aristocratic audience: the pangs of youthful love, heroic derring-do, tender lyricism and violent declamation.

The hero and heroine have been compared to Romeo and Juliet, but in the main the resemblances are superficial. The "star-crossed" lovers of Shakespeare are the helpless victims of a family feud; they are youth destroyed by the blindness and unreason of old age. Corneille's lovers too are vibrant, passionate youths, tortured by an inflexible older generation. Chimene's father, Count Gormas, who had hoped to receive the coveted post of tutor to the Prince, is passed over in favor of the older

Don Diegue, father of Rodrigue. An angry discussion between the two culminates in a mortal affront: the Count slaps the aging Diegue, who is forced to seek vengeance through his son. Rodrigue slays the Count, but in doing so forces his beloved to demand, in turn, her own vengeance, his life. Yet Rodrigue and Chimene are not helpless victims. They are fully conscious of the dilemma imposed on them, a dilemma which does not merely involve a conflict between duty and love, but a contradiction in the nature of love itself. Love in the world of Corneille involves *gloire*—one's standing in society and one's sense of personal integrity—so that love may in fact be on the side of duty. For if Rodrigue should fail to do what the code of honor demands, he would prove unworthy of Chimene.

This concept of *worthiness* is typically Cornelian, and represents the belief that the great-souled, the noble-hearted (terms which inadequately translate the adjective *généreux*) are different from ordinary men. Their passion is more sublime, and makes almost impossible demands upon lovers. Great-souledness, *générosité*, is a matter of rank; your true aristocrat has a sublimity in all his actions which sets him apart.

[1] **Gloire** and **générosité** are difficult to define today because they are essentially aristocratic in conception. It is from the viewpoint of **gloire** that all the other Cornelian "virtues," including **générosité**, are conceived. **Gloire** has different aspects: it may involve the hero's search for public esteem, his desire to take advantage of various conflicts or duties to test his strength, or a kind of self-respect oblivious to success or failure. **Générosité** characterizes the man of noble birth; it is his quality of sublimity, his ability to rise above the earthly and emotional.

It is Corneille's genius to have conceived Chimene's predicament as quite different from Rodrigue's; although for a moment she echoes him, declaring that she must seek his death to be worthy of his love, her heart is not in it. Ostensibly mistress of Rodrigue's fate, to whom, like all courtly lovers, he kneels in submission, she is actually weakened by her love, and he can force her by his almost brutal insistence on dying, to confess that she hopes her pursuit of him will fail. Her struggle is not with love's sublime values, but with its fatality; her terror is in finding that she is unable to hate the "object of her hatred." Unlike Rodrigue, she cannot freely declare her love, but must hide it, and it is against her every inclination that she demands his death. Paradoxically, until she reaches this abhorred solution, her dilemma can never be resolved. Although the play ends with the father-figure King's declaration that time will heal all, and cannot be called tragic in the Aristotelian sense, both the protagonists sense that Rodrigue must forever combine two irreconciliables: the lover, and the father's murderer. In the King's final injunction there is thus a desolate irony for the lovers; for neither time, the royal promise, nor Rodrigue's prowess can ever change this immutable fact.

A further variation on love's dilemma is provided by a secondary character, the Infanta, Doña Urraque. Critics have traditionally found her superfluous, and stage productions have frequently excised the rôle, although happily this is not the case at the Comédie Française today. Actually her gentle and melancholy presence is an important leitmotiv: Rodrigue is the greater for being loved by his prin-

cess, with whom—O sublime Cornelian delicacy!
—he exchanges not one word from beginning to
end. Her love is hopeless because of the involve-
ment of *gloire* with hierarchy. She must, to be
worthy of her position, let Chimene marry Rodrigue, who despite his renown is beneath her in
station. For the Infanta, as for Chimene, each de-
velopment in the action sharpens or complicates
the dilemma. When Rodrigue, by his prowess
against the Moors, becomes the defender of the
realm and the idol of his people, Chimene's deter-
mination opposes not only her true feelings, but
the public good. Similarly, as Rodrigue becomes
progressively more king-like with each victory, he
becomes more worthy of the Infanta's love.

At the root of the action is a conflict between two
different modes of life: a violent and uninhibited
individualism, typical of the later years of the
Renaissance, and the growing refinement and disci-
pline of the court. The fiery Count de Gormas is
squarely in opposition to the new order because
he considers himself the equal, even the superior,
of the King whose empire he has so often saved.
That Rodrigue's deed punishes Gormas' independ-
ence and rebelliousness as well as his insult to Don
Diegue goes a long way to explain the King's ready
forgiveness. For the Count resembles those powerful noblemen whom Louis XIII's prime minister,
Richelieu, was gradually stripping of power; the
recalcitrant among them were to perish, like Mont-
morency, on the scaffold. In contrast, Rodrigue sees
his victory over the Moors as a duty to the King,
to whom belongs first of all the glory of their defeat, and despite his exultation, at no time does he

forget he is his monarch's servant. Don Diegue,
though he is an obedient courtier, clings fiercely
to the code of honor which demands death for an
insult. This taking of vengeance into one's own
hands was itself an individualistic act infringing
on the royal power; Richelieu had made dueling a
capital offense. The surreptitious note in Rodrigue's
challenge to the Count reflects this official dis-
approval, as does the King's expressed repugnance
for the second duel, which he reluctantly permits
only when Chimene invokes the long-standing right
to choose a champion.

Such a skillful interweaving of themes is only
one proof of the expertness with which Corneille
constructed his play. In the process, he paid only
the most grudging heed to the Unities of Time,
Place, and Action—those famous classical rules,
based on an erroneous interpretation of Aristotle's
Art of Poetry—which required that the action of a
play be single, in one setting, and within the space
of one day. Obviously, in the *Cid*, unity of place
has the widest possible interpretation, and the play
requires the "simultaneous" stage-setting which com-
bines a city street, the entrances to various houses,
and a large palace room in the foreground, with
exits on both sides—a setting such as was recently
adopted by the Comédie Française. This arrange-
ment gives full play to the remarkably varied
rhythm and movement of what may at first seem
to the Anglo-Saxon reader a "static" drama. For
example, in the first act, three scenes each requiring
a different location are followed by three which
form a single tableau. In general, this is the pattern
of each act: a series of encounters, followed by a

tableau in which the action is summarized and discussed. Corneille himself pointed to the almost cinematographic movement of I. iii, the famous scene of the slap: "One may imagine," he wrote, "that Don Diegue and the Count, leaving the King's palace, keep on walking as they quarrel, and arrive at the former's house when he receives the slap which requires him to enter it in search of help."

Corneille compressed his action into what are perhaps the most crowded twenty-four hours in the history of drama. But the telescoping of time is a dramatic convention like any other, and should not bother the reader of Shakespeare. And Corneille compensates to some extent for the crowding by making his action encompass two days, beginning around noon, and continuing through the night and early afternoon of the following day. On re-flexion, it may still be difficult for the reader to imagine how, in addition to the other action, Rodrigue could leave the palace for the port, lie in wait for the Moors, attack and defeat them, and return in triumph to tell his tale early in Act IV. The point is, however, that a reader is not a spectator, and Corneille does not give his audience time to reflect on such matters. They are too busy feeling the *admiratio* or wonder he considered an essential element of tragedy, puzzling over what will happen next, or listening to the poetry.

For one should also approach the play as a listener. If at times the speeches seem excessively legalistic, this is due in large measure to the predicament of the characters, especially of Chimene, who must desperately conjure away the power of passion by neat if empty ratiocination. Should we feel tempted, like old Capulet, to shout "chop-logic!" we should remember that it is the desperate refuge of a hounded girl. The plainness, the prosiness of much of the language (less evident in French) highlights through contrast such passages as Rodrigue's description of his defeat of the Moors, with its chiaroscuro effects and geometric design reminiscent of Claude Lorrain, or Chimene's heartbroken speech on the death of her father, which with its baroque imagery is very close to Shakespeare (especially *Macbeth*, II. iii. 116-19). In general, the classic drama depends for much of its effect on this kind of alternance; the poetic passage is more sublime when surrounded by near-prose dialogue, just as Chimene's "Nay, I do not hate thee," after her long restraint, has twice the effect of an outright declaration of passion.

After the *Cid*, Corneille was silent four years, perhaps in discouragement at the violent critical attacks he had suffered. When he resumed writing, it was to produce tragedies with sterner themes: patriotism and civic virtue, renunciation and sacrifice. In these works of his subsequent career one can still glimpse Corneille's love of intricate situations, of surprise, of grandiose word and deed, but in none did he ever attain again the high lyricism, the sheer youthful exuberance, the heights of exultation and depths of melancholy of the *Cid*. If, despite *Médée*, we may rightly consider it his first tragedy, then he could well have said, with his hero:

Our firstling blows come down like master-strokes.

PRINCIPAL DATES IN CORNEILLE'S LIFE

✻

1606   Birth of Pierre Corneille, in Rouen, June 6.

1622   Finishes studies at the Jesuit college of Rouen.

1624   Receives law degree.

1625-29   His first play, *Mélite,* a comedy, staged in Paris.

1632   *Clitandre,* tragicomedy.

1633-34   Three comedies, *La Veuve, La Galerie du Palais,* and *La Suivante. Médée,* a tragedy.

1636   *L'Illusion comique,* comedy, and *Le Cid,* tragicomedy, based on the play by Guillen de Castro, *Las Mocedades del Cid.* Richelieu grants him an annual pension of 1,500 livres.

1637-38   "Quarrel of the Cid," various critics and the Academy itself publish criticisms, to which the author replies.

1640   *Horace* and *Cinna,* tragedies. Marriage to Marie de Lampérière.

1641-43   *Polyeucte,* tragedy.

1642-43   *La Mort de Pompée,* tragedy; *le Menteur,* comedy; *la Suite du Menteur,* comedy.

1644   *Rodogune*, tragedy.

1645   *Théodore, vierge et martyre*, tragedy.

1647   *Héraclius*, tragedy.

1650   *Andromède*, tragedy "with machines" (the use of stage machinery for spectacular effects, as in opera), *Don Sanche d'Aragon*, heroic comedy.

1651   *Nicomède*, tragedy.

1652   *Pertharite*, tragedy which fails. Corneille gives up writing drama for seven years.

1659   Returns to the theatre with *Œdipe*, tragedy.

1661   *La Toison d'Or*, tragedy with machines.

1662   *Sertorius*, tragedy.

1663   *Sophonisbe*, tragedy.

1664   *Othon*, tragedy.

1666   *Agésilas*, tragedy.

1667   *Attila*, tragedy.

1670   *Tite et Bérénice*, heroic comedy.

1671   *Psyché*, tragic ballet, in collaboration with Molière, Quinault, and Lully.

1672   *Pulchérie*, heroic comedy.

1684   Death of Corneille on October 1st.

DRAMATIS PERSONAE

※

DON FERNAND	King of Castille
DOÑA URRAQUE	Infanta of Castille
DON DIEGUE	father of Don Rodrigue
DON GOMES	Count de Gormas, father of Chimene
DON RODRIGUE	in love with Chimene
DON SANCHE	suitor of Chimene
DON ARIAS DON ALONSE	} Castilian noblemen
CHIMENE	daughter of Don Gomes
LEONOR	lady in waiting to the Infanta
ELVIRE	lady in waiting to Chimene
A PAGE	

SCENE: *Seville*[2]

[Note. The names of the characters should be pronounced as in French, with the accent on the last syllable, e.g., Rodrigue, Row-*dreeg;* Chimene, Shee-*main;* Diegue, D'yegg; Sanche, Sawnsh; Leonor, Lay-oh-*norr*].

[2] Seville in Andalusia, on the Guadalquivir River.

LE CID

Act I

❦

SCENE I

[Enter CHIMENE *and* ELVIRE*]*

CHIMENE.   Elvire, is your report indeed a true
   one?
Have you concealed none of my father's words?
   ELVIRE.   His words brought a delight that still I
   feel;
For Rodrigue his esteem equals your adoration,
And if I do not err, reading his thoughts,   5
He will command you to return his love.
   CHIMENE.   Tell me again, I pray you, once again,
How he approves my choice, what are my hopes;
Such sweet discourse ne'er wearies in the telling,
And I could hear forever your great promise   10
That now our love may freely stand revealed
To the bright day. And tell me, did you say
How Sanche and Don Rodrigue seek your support
As rivals to my hand. Did you disclose
My preference?
   ELVIRE.   I showed your heart unmoved   15
By these two suitors, granting neither one
Hope or despair; I told him you refuse
To frown or smile on either, but await
In dutiful submission his command

1

20 To make your choice. This filial respect
   Delighted him; his looks, his words gave proof
   Of his delight, and since I must relate
   Once more his words, here then is how he spoke:
   "She knows her duty, and of such a bride
25 Each man is worthy, each from noble line,
   Valiant and faithful, springs, and though so young,
   Their glances show the valor of their race.
   Young Don Rodrigue has a most noble countenance
   In every feature speaks the man of courage;
30 He springs from a line of mighty warriors,
   All of them born 'midst plaudits and acclaim.
   His doughty father, champion in his time,
   Until his strength forsook him, marvels wrought,
   Each line upon his brow tells some great deed
35 Of former days, and now this worthy son
   Of worthy father seeks to wed Chimene:
   Here is my word: I shall their love approve."
   Here he cut off his speech; the time was pressing,
   The council chamber called. But these few words,
40 However brief, reveal no hesitancy
   Between your suitors. The King must choose today
   A tutor for his son, and to your father
   By right shall fall this most exalted post.
   The choice is certain, for so rare a valor
45 Cannot permit that we should fear a rival.
   Your lover's father, at his son's request,
   Leaving the council, will propose the match.
   Judge then, from this, that he'll choose well his
        moment,
   And soon your every wish will be contented.
     CHIMENE.   Yet it does seem my strangely troubled
50   spirit
   Will not share in this joy, but is perturbed;

A moment can alter the face of destiny;
So, in my happiness, I fear misfortune.
> ELVIRE.   Your fears, believe me, shall unfounded
>   prove.
> CHIMENE.   Let us await what way our fate shall
>   move.   [*Exeunt*] 55

SCENE II

[Enter the INFANTA *and* LEONOR, *with a* PAGE]

> INFANTA.   Page, go at once, and tell Chimene it
>   grieves me

That she does wait so long e'er she comes to me.
> LEONOR.   Madam, each day the same desire o'er-
>   whelms you,

Each day, when you converse with her, you ask
How her love fares, what progress it has made.   5
> INFANTA.   I have a reason, for 'twas I who forced
>   her

To bare her breast before the shafts of love;
She loves Rodrigue; 'twas I who gave him to her,
And I who helped him vanquish her disdain
And so, having bound the lovers in their chains,   10
It is my interest that their love should prosper.
> LEONOR.   Yet, Madam, when their love succeeds,
>   you show

Not joy, but deep distress. Can it be true
This passion, overwhelming them with joy,
Brings only sorrow to your noble heart?   15
Does the great interest that you take in them
Make you unhappy at their happiness?
But I go too far; pardon my indiscretion.
> INFANTA.   My sorrows double when I keep them
>   hidden.

20 Listen, and I shall tell how I have fought;
   Pity my weakness and admire my strength.
   The tyrant love spares no one; this young knight,
   This valiant lover, whom I shall give in marriage,
   I love him.
     LEONOR.   You love him?
     INFANTA.   Lay your hand here, I pray you,
25 Upon my breast, feel how the heart beats fast
   To hear its conqueror's name.
     LEONOR.   Forgive me, Madam,
   If I o'erstep the deep respect I owe you,
   But how can a princess so forget her rank,
   That she could love a simple cavalier?
30 What would the king say, what would Castille say?
   Have you forgotten who your father is?
     INFANTA.   So little have I forgot it, I would shed
   My royal blood, to keep my rank unblemished.
   Let me remind you that in noble hearts
35 Merit alone may kindle rightful love;
   And should my passion seek excuse, I'd find
   Most noble precedents. But when my honor,
   When pride of birth's at stake, I shall not falter,
   My will stands firm against the senses' shocks;
40 Pride teaches me, a monarch's child, this lesson:
   None but a king is worthy of my hand.
   I gave another what I dared not take,
   Freeing myself, I bound Chimene in chains;
   Lighting their passion's fire, put out my own.
45 So do not wonder that my tortured soul
   Awaits their marriage all impatiently;
   You know my peace of mind depends upon it.
   Love lives on hope, love dies when hope is dead.
   Love is a flame that wanes for want of fuel.

Despite the rigors of this sad adventure,   50
If once Chimene takes Don Rodrigue as husband,
My hopes are dead, my wounded spirit healed.
Meantime, my torment is beyond conception.
Until her marriage, I shall love Rodrigue,
I strive to lose him, yet the loss is bitter;   55
There lies the source of my concealed distress.
Alas, I know the power of love to rule me,
To make me sigh for him that I must scorn;
Though strong my will, my spirit's torn in twain,
I fear this marriage, yet do I desire it.   60
Whatever comes, I cannot hope for joy,
For love and honor tug at me so fiercely
That I shall die if it take place or not.
   LEONOR.   Madam, now I know all, I can say no
     more,
Save that I too feel grief at your misfortune.   65
A moment hence I blamed you, now I pity you.
But since you arm yourself against an evil
Both sweet and virulent, since you do battle
'Gainst both its charms and powers, hold at bay
Its fierce assaults, rejecting all temptation,   70
So shall your virtue calm your stormy heart.
Place all your hopes in this, in healing time,
And Heaven's kindness, for it is too just
To abandon virtue to an endless grief.
   INFANTA.   My dearest hope is that I may lose
     hope.   75

[*Enter the* PAGE]

   PAGE.   Lady, at your command Chimene awaits
     you.
   INFANTA.   [*To* LEONOR]

Go, speak to her a moment in the hallway.
>   LEONOR.   Will you remain here, Madam, with
>   your thoughts?
>   INFANTA.   No, give me but a moment to com-
>   pose
80 My face, and hide my sorrows; when 'tis done
I'll follow you.   [*Exit* LEONOR]
>   Just Heaven, source of my help,
End, end, I pray, the sickness that destroys me,
Grant me repose, help me assure my honor,
I place in others' joy my own good fortune;
85 Not only two, but three hearts seek this wedding,
O hasten it, or give me greater powers.
Once they are joined in wedlock these my chains
Will break asunder, and my torment cease.
But I delay too long, I must seek Chimene,
90 And quell my grief in talk with her again.   [*Exit*]

SCENE III

[*Enter the* COUNT *and* DON DIEGUE]

>   THE COUNT.   So then, you've won, and by the
>   royal favor,
>   Rise to an office that was mine by right;
>   You are named tutor to the Prince.
>   DON DIEGUE.   The King
>   Thus honoring all my house, displayed his justice,
> 5 Did amply demonstrate how he rewards
>   Past services.
>   THE COUNT.   However great they be,
>   Kings are but men, and have men's weaknesses;
>   Like other men, they make mistakes, and this
> 10 Proves to us courtiers what scant rewards

They offer present services.
   Don Diegue.   Enough,
Let's say no more of a choice that does offend you,
Bestowed perhaps as much for love as merit.
But to the absolute power of a king
We owe too much respect to question him   15
In aught he does. I beg you, to this honor,
Add still another; join by sacred ties
My house to yours. You have an only daughter,
I have an only son, and with their marriage,
We shall become forever more than friends.   20
   The Count. This precious son ought to aim
      higher still,
And the new brilliance of your great position
Should fill his heart with loftier aspirations.
Be tutor, Sir, and teach the Prince to reign
Over a province, show him how to make   25
A nation in his power quake with terror,
Swell the good hearts with love, the bad with fear.
To all these skills, conjoin a captain's virtue,
Show him how he must harden to misfortune,
How in the game of war he must be matchless,   30
Spend entire days and nights on horseback, sleep
Wearing full armor. Teach him to storm a wall,
To turn the tide of battle by himself;
Teach him, by your example, till he's perfect,
Show by your deeds your lessons were well taught.   35
   Don Diegue. To teach him by example, I need
      only
Tell him to read the story of my life.
Reading that lengthy list of valiant deeds
He'd swiftly learn how one may conquer nations,
Attack a fortress, or command an army,   40

Thus, upon deeds, build high his right to fame.
   THE COUNT.   Living examples speak with louder
      voice,
A prince ill learns his duty in a book,
And after all, what have your years produced
45 That in one day of battle, I'd not equal?
Once you were brave, but I am brave today.
This arm defends the kingdom, this bright sword
Sets Aragon, Grenada, all a-tremble.
My name alone's a bulwark of Castille.
50 Were I not here, you would have other masters,
Soon you would languish under enemy rule.
Each day, each instant sees my glory grow,
Laurel on laurel, conquest on conquest heaped.
At my side, the Prince could try his strength in
      battle,
55 Shielded by my strong arm, he'd learn to conquer
Watching me conquer; and soon he would fulfill
His noble promise, he would see . . .
   DON DIEGUE.   I know,
You serve your monarch well. I have seen you fight,
And lead your troops while under my command.
60 When age had poured its ice into my veins,
Your peerless valor took the place of mine.
In short, to spare unnecessary speech,
Today you are what I was formerly.
However, as you see, in the present contest,
65 The King between us still makes some distinction.
   THE COUNT.   No; you have taken what was mine
      by right.
   DON DIEGUE.   He who has won it from you most
      deserved it.
   THE COUNT.   He who best fills the post is the
      more worthy.

DON DIEGUE. To be refused is scarcely proof of
   merit.

THE COUNT. You, an old courtier, won it
   through intrigue.   70

DON DIEGUE. My brightly shining deeds were
   my sole spokesmen.

THE COUNT. Say rather that the King honors
   your years.

DON DIEGUE. When the King grants honors, 'tis
   for courage only.

THE COUNT. Then this honor of yours was due
   to me alone.

DON DIEGUE. He who did not receive it, was
   unworthy.   75

THE COUNT. Unworthy! I?

DON DIEGUE.   You.

THE COUNT.   Your insolence,
You rash old fool, now reaps its just reward.
                          [*He slaps him*]

DON DIEGUE. [*Drawing his sword*]
Go on, end my life, for this affront has set
The first blush of shame upon my race's brow.

THE COUNT. What can you hope to do, weak as
   you are?   [*He disarms him*] 80

DON DIEGUE. O God! My strength deserts me in
   my need,

THE COUNT. Your sword is mine, but you would
   be too vain,
If my hand should ever touch so poor a trophy;
Now go and tell the Prince to read your story;
To such a tale, so just a punishment   85
Will add, I vow, no mean embellishment.   [*Exit*]

Scene IV

Don Diegue.   O rage! O despair! O villainous
      old age!
'Tis for such infamy I have lived so long,
To see the laurels wither in one day
Upon this hair grown white in the heat of battle.
5 My arm, the wonder of admiring Spain,
My arm, so many times the Empire's saviour,
So many times the throne's support, today
Abandons me, betrays me in my struggle!
O cruel memory of glories past!
10 The toil of years rubbed out in one brief day.
My proud new rank has overturned my fortunes,
From that high precipice my honor's fallen.
Shall I allow the Count to dim its splendor,
Die unavenged, or live a life of shame?
15 Ay, Count, you should be tutor to the Prince,
For this high post does spurn a man disgraced,
And your fierce jealousy, your base affront,
Though the King thought me fit, prove me un-
      worthy.
And thou, my sword, the glorious instrument
20 Of my great deeds, useless to one whose blood
Flows cold as ice, once thou wert feared, but now,
Thou'rt but a bauble. So then, I put thee off,
And now, the least of men, no more shall wear thee,
But give thee unto hands worthy to bear thee!

Scene V

[*Enter* Rodrigue]

Rodrigue, are you courageous?
      Rodrigue.   Such a question

From any but my father, would be answered
By my sword.
    DON DIEGUE.   Sweet anger, welcome fire! Your
        rage
In my distress, recalls what race is mine;   5
My youth lives once again in your wrath's quick
        flame.
Go, my true son, go and efface my shame,
Avenge me.
    RODRIGUE. In what cause?
    DON DIEGUE.   So great an outrage,
It deals a mortal blow to both our honors,   10
A slap. It would have cost the wretch his life,
Had not my years betrayed my noble urge.
This sword that my poor arm no more can bear,
I put in yours to avenge me, and to punish
The arrogant foe on whom you'll try your courage. 15
Only his blood can wash away the insult,
Kill him, or die. But mark you well my words,
Your adversary is a man of mettle,
One I have watched all smeared with blood and
        dust,
Spread terror through whole armies. I have seen 20
Him rout a hundred squadrons with his valor,
And, to hide nothing from you, more than brave,
More than a valiant captain, this man is . . .
    RODRIGUE. Speak, speak, I pray you!
    DON DIEGUE.   Father to Chimene.
    RODRIGUE. Father . . .   25
    DON DIEGUE.   No more; I know how
        much you love her.
But he who lives disgraced, deserves to die;
When the offender's dear, the offense is greater;
You know the wrong, what vengeance it demands,

I'll say no more. Take my revenge and yours,
30 Prove you a worthy son of worthy father.
Bowed 'neath the sorrow fate inflicts upon me,
I go to weep alone. But haste, to vengeance!

[*Exit*]

Scene VI

RODRIGUE. Now does sharp grief pierce through
    my heart,
And, without warning, make its mortal thrust;
Helpless avenger in a cause most just,
Pitiful victim of the Fates' cruel art;
5   I cannot move, and my poor heart brought low,
    Weakens beneath the blow.
This day were we to join our loves together,
    O God! the fearful pain!
For in this quarrel, the victim is my father,
10 And his traducer, father to Chimene!

    O, the fierce struggle in my soul!
Against my honor, my love pleads its case;
Avenge my father? Flee my love's embrace?
One hinders me, one spurs me to my goal.
15   This is my bitter choice: my love betray,
    Or shun the light of day.
In either course, my torment will be long;
    O God! the fearful pain!
Then I must leave unpunished this deep wrong?
20 I must destroy the father of Chimene?

    Father, or loved one, honor or love,
Most noble rigor, dearest tyranny;
Pleasure must die, or honor stainèd be;
I must be wretched, or a coward prove.

To wield thee, sword, my noble heart aspires,   25
    Yet still feels passion's fires;
Before thee, worthy blade, my joys have fled;
    Sword that inflicts such pain,
Have I received thee to avenge my blood,
Have I received thee to betray Chimene?   30

    No, let me die; have I not sworn
Allegiance to my loved one quite as great
As to my father? I shall gain her hate
If I avenge him; if I do not, her scorn.
    Whatever course I take, I cease to love her,   35
    Or prove unworthy of her.
My malady grows worse when I would cure it;
    All things increase my pain,
Well then, since I must die, be strong, my spirit!
And let me perish faithful to Chimene.   40

    What, die without redress!
What, seek a death so fatal to my fame!
Permit the realm to brand me with the shame
Of one who ill defends his ancient race,
    All for a love my heart, so tempest-tossed,   45
    Knows is forever lost?
I shall not heed this base and subtle plea
    That only sharpens pain;
Come then, my arm, at least keep honor free,
Since when all's done, I must lose my Chimene.   50

    'Tis true, my spirit was unsure.
To my father, not my lover, I owe all,
Whether I die of grief, or in combat fall,
I'll cleanse our sullied blood, till it be pure
    As once it was. Too long unmanned am I,   55

I must to vengeance fly!
Weigh nothing more, lament no more, but rather,
    Refuse to feel such pain
That in this quarrel, the victim is my father,
60 And his traducer, father to Chimene.

Act II

Scene I

[*Enter the* Count *and* Don Arias]

THE COUNT. I do confess I was too hot of blood,
I took too strong exception to a word;
Between us, I went too far. But what's done is done.
  DON ARIAS. Then let your great heart yield to
      the King's command;
He is deeply moved, and should you anger him, 5
He might bring down upon you all his power.
What's more, you have no strong defence in the
      matter—
The victim's rank, the boldness of the outrage
Cry loudly for submission and repentance
Beyond the usual bounds of satisfaction. 10
  THE COUNT. My life or death hang on the
      King's command.
  DON ARIAS. Thus violence follows hard upon
      offense.
The King still loves you, you must quell his wrath.
He has said "I so command;" will you not obey?
  THE COUNT. Sir, to preserve the esteem men
      hold me in, 15
To disobey a little were no crime;
And if it were, my present services
Are great enough the King should overlook it.
  DON ARIAS. However great and glorious be our
      exploits,

15

20 No king is e'er indebted to a subject;
This is self-flattery; you surely know
That he who serves his king does but his duty.
Such trust in your own power may cost you dear.
    THE COUNT. I shall believe you when it comes
        to pass.
    DON ARIAS. You ought to fear the power of a
25   king.
    THE COUNT. I shall outlive a single day's dis-
        pleasure.
Let the whole state take arms to bring me down,
If I must perish, Spain herself shall fall.
    DON ARIAS. What? You fear so little the sover-
        eign might . . .
    THE COUNT. Of one who, lacking my support,
30   would lose
His scepter? No, my person is too precious,
And should my head fall, so his crown would fall.
    DON ARIAS. Take, I beseech you, reason as your
        guide,
Resolve. . . .
35   THE COUNT. My firm resolve's already made.
    DON ARIAS. What shall I tell the King? I must
        report.
    THE COUNT. That I shall ne'er consent to my
        own disgrace.
    DON ARIAS. Remember, a king expects entire
        obedience.
    THE COUNT. Dear Sir, the die is cast, let's say
        no more.
    DON ARIAS. Farewell then, since I cannot change
40   your purpose.
Beware, for even laurels are no proof
Against the lightning.

THE COUNT.   Well, I shall await it
Quite unafraid.
    DON ARIAS.   Soon you may feel its blast.
    THE COUNT.   Why then, Don Diegue would be
       content, at last.   [*Exit* DON ARIAS]   45
The heart that fears not death, need not fear threats,
My courage towers o'er the cruelest fate.
I could be forced to live unloved, or poor,
But life dishonored I could ne'er endure.

SCENE II

[*Enter* DON RODRIGUE]

    DON RODRIGUE.   Your Grace, a word with you.
    THE COUNT.   Say on.
    DON RODRIGUE.   Relieve me
Of a doubt. You know Don Diegue?
    THE COUNT.   I do.
    DON RODRIGUE.   Speak softly,
And hear my words. Know you that this old man
Was honor, manhood, bravery, all in one?
    THE COUNT.   Perhaps.   5
    DON RODRIGUE.   Know you that in my an-
       gry glance
'Tis his blood speaks?
    THE COUNT.   What matters it to me?
    DON RODRIGUE.   Four paces off I'll teach you
       what it matters.
    THE COUNT.   You rash young fool!
    DON RODRIGUE.   Speak calmly. I am young,
'Tis true; but in those of valiant lineage,
Valor waits not upon the years.   10
    THE COUNT.   But you

Measure yourself 'gainst me! whence comes such
    vanity
In one who has never yet borne arms?
   Don Rodrigue.   My kind
Require no second chance to make their mark.
Our firstling blows come down like master strokes.
15   The Count. But know you who I am?
   Don Rodrigue.   Yes. Any other
Would shake with fright at the mere sound of your
    name.
Writ large upon the laurels at your brow,
I seem to read the promise of my death.
Boldly I face a champion yet unconquered,
Yet shall not want for strength, for my heart is
20   strong;
You are unvanquished, not invincible.
   The Count. The heart that speaks so bravely
    in these words,
Each day I watched shine brighter in your gaze;
And seeing in you the honor of Castille,
25 With joyous heart, I promised you my daughter.
I know your love. I am well pleased to see
Your passion yield to duty. Your proud spirit
Stands firm against all amorous assaults,
And stoutly proves it merits my esteem.
30 When I sought for a perfect knight and gentleman
As son-in-law, my choice falling on you,
Was not misplaced. Yet now I pity you,
Admire your courage, and lament your youth.
In your first trial of arms, pursue not death,
35 Spare me the shame of an unequal combat,
Such easy victory would bring scant honor,
To win unperiled is an empty triumph.
The world would think it easy to have slain you,

I would reap only sorrow from your death.
    DON RODRIGUE.   Thus scornful pity follows upon
        outrage: 40
You steal my honor, yet fear to take my life?
    THE COUNT.   Get you gone.
    DON RODRIGUE.   Enough, let us go forth at once.
    THE COUNT.   Are you so tired of life?
    DON RODRIGUE.   Do you fear death?
    THE COUNT.   Come, then, you do your duty; he
        is base
Who can survive his father's deep disgrace.   45
                            [*Exeunt*]

SCENE III

[*Enter* CHIMENE, *the* INFANTA, *and* LEONOR]

INFANTA.   Restrain your sorrow, do not weep,
    Chimene,
In this unhappy hour, keep your soul strong.
Your skies will clear, 'tis but a passing tempest,
Only a tiny cloud obscures your fortunes,
Happiness is not lost, 'tis but delayed.   5
    CHIMENE.   My heart, worn by its woes, dares not
    take hope,
Such sudden storms, ruffling a tranquil sea,
Do threaten our frail bark, that she will sink
Here in the harbor, 'ere she can set sail.
I loved, was loved, our fathers had agreed,   10
But at the very moment I related
Our wondrous story, they had fallen to quarreling,
So to destroy our dearest expectation.
Cursed ambition, O, that hateful madness,
Whose tyranny the noblest spirits suffer,   15
Cruel honor, you have ruined all my hopes,
What tears, what sighs you keep in store for me!

INFANTA. But you have naught to fear from
their dispute;
It flared in an instant, and will as quickly die,
20 'Tis too well known not to be reconciled;
The King already strives to make peace between
them.
And you know well, your sorrow has so distressed
me,
I'll do the impossible to end your grief.
CHIMENE. Nothing can mend their quarrel, such
wounds are mortal,
25 Prudence may plead, power command in vain,
No healing balm shall e'er reach deep enough;
The hidden fires of hatred burn the brighter
For being covered.
INFANTA. Nay, when you are wed,
That sacred bond will end your parents' hatred,
30 And drown their discord in the hymns of love.
CHIMENE. So do I wish it, yet I fear to hope,
Don Diegue is haughty, and I know my father,
I would hold back my tears, yet they will flow,
The past torments me, yet I fear the future.
INFANTA. What do you fear? An old man's fee-
35 ble arm?
CHIMENE. Rodrigue's courageous.
INFANTA. But he is too young.
CHIMENE. He was born a hero; his first blow
will prove it.
INFANTA. And yet you should not fear him over-
much,
One word from you would swiftly damp his ardor
40 He is too much in love to wish you harm.
CHIMENE. If he should not obey, what depths
of anguish!

And if he should, what will men say of him?
Born of such blood, can he endure this outrage?
Whether he yields, or spurns the pleas of love,
Shame or distress are mine, whiche'er he does: 45
My bidding, or the horrid work of vengeance.

    INFANTA.   Thus do the great-souled rise above
        their interest,
Chimene can bear no thought that hints of base-
        ness;
But if I took, until this quarrel is mended,
Your perfect knight a prisoner, so to wall up   50
His courage, would your heart then still be sore?

    CHIMENE.   Oh, Madam, then my cares would be
        no more!

[*Enter a* PAGE]

    INFANTA.   Page, find Don Rodrigue, and bring
        him to me.

    PAGE.   The Count and he . . .

    CHIMENE.   O God! I shake with fright.

    INFANTA.   Well, speak!   55

    PAGE.   Together they have left the palace.

    INFANTA.   Alone?

    PAGE.   Alone, and quarreling in low tones.

    CHIMENE.   They've come to blows; all words are
        useless now,
Madam, forgive my haste, but I must go.   [*Exit*]

SCENE IV

    INFANTA.   Alas, how my poor heart is ill at ease!
I grieve for her, her lover's charms possess me,
Calmness deserts me, passion burns anew,
New hope and sorrow, out of their separation,
Grow green and fresh, and on this lovers' parting, 5

I gaze in anguish, yet in secret joy.
    LEONOR.   Can your proud soul, so staunchly res-
        olute,
So quickly yield to an unworthy flame?
    INFANTA.   Say not unworthy, now that in my
        heart,
10 It sits enthroned in full triumphant splendor.
Speak of it with respect, 'tis dear to me,
My pride resists it, yet I dare to hope.
My heart, succumbing to this foolish dream,
Flies in pursuit of a love Chimene has lost.
    LEONOR.   So then, your firm resolve has failed,
15   and reason
No longer rules you?
    INFANTA.   Ah, how weak is reason,
When such sweet poison has enflamed the heart!
And when the patient loves her malady,
How loth she is to let herself be cured!
    LEONOR.   Your hopes are sweet, your illness
20   shuns its cure,
But this Rodrigue's unworthy of your hand.
    INFANTA.   I know it well, mayhap my will grows
        feeble,
Yet hear how love stirs hope in loving hearts:
If Don Rodrigue should prove victorious,
25 If this great warrior falls beneath his steel,
Then can I love him, cherish him unashamed.
What ways are barred him if he slays the Count?
Now I can picture entire kingdoms falling
Before his feeblest efforts, now I see him,
30 (Or so my amorous fantasy portrays him)
Seated upon the throne of great Grenada,
The beaten Moors prostrate themselves before him,

A vanquished Aragon welcomes her new con-
    queror,
Portugal bows before him, and his exploits
Reach far beyond the seas to spread his fame,   35
And bathe his laurels in the Afric blood.
In short, all that is sung of famous warriors,
After this victory, men will sing of him.
And thus shall Don Rodrigue deserve my love.
  LEONOR. But Madam, seé how far you lead his
      actions,   40
After a contest that may not take place!
  INFANTA. Rodrigue's attacked, the Count is his
      offender,
They have gone forth together, need one say more?
  LEONOR. Well, then, they'll fight, since you're
      persuaded of it;
But will Rodrigue go as far as you have dreamed? 45
  INFANTA. Bear with me, I am mad, my thoughts
      run wild;
You see what ills love keeps in store for me,
Come to my room and my consoler be.   [*Exeunt*]

SCENE V

[*Enter* DON FERNAND, DON ARIAS *and* DON SANCHE]

  DON FERNAND. Is the Count so foolish, so puffed
      up with pride,
He dares to think his crime excusable?
  DON ARIAS. Sire, I did entreat him in your
      name,
I spoke with him at length, to no avail.

DON FERNAND.   Just Heavens! A subject thus
5   defies his King,
And scorns to please him! I like not such boldness.
Thus he insults Don Diegue and flouts his ruler:
Here in my court, 'tis he who frames the laws!
Brave warrior, great commander though he be,
10 I shall know how to curb his haughty spirit;
Were he valor itself, or the great god of battles,
He shall regret the crime of disobedience.
Despite the insolence of his offense,
I did at first attempt to treat him gently,
15 But since he mocks my kindness, let him be seized,
If he resists, why then, use force to take him.
     DON SANCHE.   Perhaps with time these rebel
     fires will wane,
Your envoy found him seething with his quarrel,
And Sire, a noble heart is slow to yield
20 When in the grasp of strong emotions held.
He knows his wrong, but in his lofty pride,
Cannot unbend to ask his King's forgiveness.
     DON FERNAND.   Silence, Don Sanche, let this my
     warning be:
Whoever takes his part, shares in his crime.
     DON SANCHE.   Sire, I shall obey, but pray you,
25   grant
One word in his defense.
     DON FERNAND.   What can you say?
     DON SANCHE.   That he who dwells in the realm
     of noble deeds
Cannot descend to acts of base submission.
For him there's no surrender that's not shameless;
30 'Gainst that base word alone the Count resists.
The task you set him is too rigorous,
Had he less courage, then would he obey you.

But should you order that his warlike arm
Redeem his insult in the clash of steel,
Then, Sire, would he obey; until such order　　　35
This sword's his warrant.
　　DON FERNAND.　　　　　Your impertinence
I shall forgive, nor punish youthful ardor.
A king learns prudence, and knows worthier causes
To spill his subjects' blood. E'en as the head
Must guard the limbs that serve it, so shall he　　　40
Guard and conserve the lives of all his people.
So then, to me, your reason is no reason,
You speak as a soldier, I must act the king.
Whate'er he says, whate'er he dares to think,
Should he obey, his honor cannot suffer.　　　45
What's more, I too am injured; he disgraces
The tutor I have chosen for my son.
Attacking him, he points his blade at me,
And so defies my high authority.
But no more of this. Ten vessels we have sighted,　　　50
Flying the flag of our old enemy,
They have dared to sail as far as the river's mouth.
　　DON ARIAS.　Perforce the Moors have learned to
　　　　know you well,
So oft defeated, they have lost the heart
To challenge once again so great a conqueror.　　　55
　　DON FERNAND.　Yet still with jealous eye they
　　　　see my scepter
Ruling o'er Andalusia; this fair land
That they possessed too long. 'Gainst their desires,
That closely I could watch them, and forestall,
With all despatch, whate'er they might attempt,　　　60
These ten years past my throne has been Seville.
　　DON ARIAS.　And they have learned, in losing
　　　　their best captains,

Your kingly person's victory's guarantor;
So you have naught to fear.
    Don Fernand.   Nor to neglect.
65 Excess of confidence itself breeds danger,
And well you know how easily with the tide,
Their ships may sail up to our very walls.
Still, the report's in doubt, and I am loth
To spread in people's hearts an aimless panic.
70 A vain alarm at night would sow confusion
Throughout the city. Nay, it is enough;
Tonight let the guard be doubled on the ramparts,
And in the harbor.

[Enter Don Alonse]

    Don Alonse.   Sire, the Count is dead.
Don Diegue, by his son's hand, has ta'en his venge-
75   ance.
    Don Fernand. When I first knew the offense, I
      did foresee
The vengeance, and in vain I strove to halt it.
    Don Alonse. Chimene, in tears, comes to seek
      audience,
And would, prostrate before you, beg for justice.
    Don Fernand.   However much my heart feels
80   pity for her,
Meseems the Count deserved this punishment
For such an outrage. Yet however just
May be his death, I cannot help but mourn him,
So brave he was, so long his services,
85 So oft he shed his blood for king and state,
Despite the wilful pride that I condemn,
His loss enfeebles me, his death afflicts me.

SCENE VI

[*Enter* CHIMENE *and* DON DIEGUE]

CHIMENE. Sire, justice! justice!
DON DIEGUE. Sire, hear both our pleas.
CHIMENE. I kneel before you, Sire.
DON DIEGUE. I clasp your knees.
CHIMENE. I beg for justice.
DON DIEGUE. I plead his defense.
CHIMENE. Punish the crime of this presump-
    tuous youth,
He has cut off your scepter's chief support; 5
He has slain my father.
DON DIEGUE. But avenged his own.
CHIMENE. The King owes justice to his subjects'
    blood.
DON DIEGUE. To take one's just revenge is not
    a crime.
DON FERNAND. I pray you, both arise; speak
    each in turn.
Chimene, I grieve for you in your misfortune, 10
My heart is stricken with an equal pain.
(*To* DON DIEGUE)
You shall speak later; hear first her lament.
CHIMENE. O Sire, my father's dead, these eyes
    have seen
The blood in great drops gush from his noble flank,
The blood that has so oft preserved our ramparts, 15
The blood that has so many battles won.
That blood, as it poured out, still smoked with
    anger,
That it should flow for any but yourself.
In spite of dangers, war had never shed it,

20 Yet here, on royal ground, Rodrigue has spilled it.
   All weak and pale I hastened to the place,
   I found him lifeless. Sire, pardon me,
   My too great grief does choke my voice with tears,
   And leaves me only sobs to speak my sorrow.
       DON FERNAND.   Have courage, child, and know
25   that from this day,
   Your king will be a father in his place.
       CHIMENE.   Ah, Sire, you crown my grief with
          too much honor.
   But I have said, I found him lifeless, Sire.
   His wounds gaped open, and to shock me more,
30 His blood wrote out my duty in the dust,
   Rather, to stir my failing heart, his valor,
   Spoke through his wounds and urged me on to
          vengeance,
   And to this audience with a most just king.
   Now those sad lips beseech you with my voice:
35 You must not suffer, Sire, under your rule
   Licence to flourish thus before your eyes,
   The bravest men to fall to some chance blow
   Dealt in sheer boldness; and presumptuous youths
   To triumph over heroes, and unpunished,
40 Bathe in their blood, make mockery of their fame.
   Seeing so brave a captain unavenged,
   Must surely damp the zeal of those who serve you.
   Enough, my father's dead, I call for vengeance,
   More for your sake than to appease my anger,
45 Such a great loss is above all the King's.
   Strike, not for me, but for your scepter's sake,
   For majesty, for the honor of your person.
   Strike, Sire, I beg you, for the good of the realm,
   So to destroy all pride in such a crime.
50   DON FERNAND.   Don Diegue, 'tis yours to speak.

Don Diegue. O, he is happy
Who loses life when all his strength is spent.
For what bleak fate awaits the valiant heart
That still beats on, after long years have passed!
I, whose long labors had won so much glory,
Who long ago had victory in my train, 55
Today have lived too long, for I must bear
A savage blow, yet can make no defense.
The hurt no combat dealt, nor siege nor ambush,
Nor all Grenada's might and Aragon's,
Nor all my foes, nor all the envious throng, 60
Almost before your eyes the Count has dealt me,
Hating your choice, and proud of the advantage
Old age had given him o'er me. Sire, this head,
Grown white beneath the helm of war, this blood,
So often shed for you, and for the state, 65
This arm, that once struck fear in enemy hearts,
Had to the grave gone down besmirched with
    shame,
But lo, I had a son of father worthy,
Of country and of king. He lent his arm,
He killed the Count and so restored my honor, 70
Washing away my shame. If it be outrage
Thus to make proof of courage when we're injured,
If to avenge this blow deserves chastisement,
The crime's my own, and on my head comes down
The lightning-bolt. When the hand errs, the head 75
Must bear the blame, and if this be a crime,
Then, Sire, I am the head, he but the hand.
Chimene complains Rodrigue has slain her father,
Could I have dealt the blow, he would be blame-
    less,
Take then this life, whose tide is ebbing fast, 80
Spare a young arm that still can serve you well.

Let my blood flow, and so appease Chimene;
I'll gladly suffer death, nor shall resist
Such dire decree, for if today I die
85 I die content, to die without dishonor.
    DON FERNAND. The matter's grave and must be
        gravely thought on
In solemn council. Sanche, conduct Chimene
To her home. Don Diegue, your word that you will
    make
My court your prison. Bring his son before me.
[*To both*]
90 You shall have justice.
    CHIMENE.   Sire, the laws demand
A murderer shall perish for his crime.
    DON FERNAND. Seek in repose, my child, sur-
        cease of sorrow,
    CHIMENE. Such a command brings but increase
        of sorrow.

Act III

Scene I

[Enter ELVIRE *and* RODRIGUE*]*

ELVIRE.   Rodrigue! What folly's here, O wretched
  man!

RODRIGUE.   Thus follow I the course of my sad
  fate.

ELVIRE.   But whence such boldness, such outrage renew'd,

Thus to profane a house you shroud in black,

Thus to defy the dead Count's very shade? 5

Was he not slain by you?

RODRIGUE.   Living, he shamed me.

'Twas honor did command that I should slay him.

 ELVIRE.   But to seek shelter in the victim's house,

Did e'er assassin covet such a refuge?

RODRIGUE.   I only come to kneel before my
  judge, 10

Turn not upon me these astonished looks,

I who have slain, come here in search of justice.

My judge will be my lover, sweet Chimene.

Alone to earn her hatred merits death,

And I have come to beg a sovereign boon: 15

To hear her lips condemn me, and to die.

 ELVIRE.   To flee her sight, her anger, were more
  prudent.

Hide rather from the first hot flush of rage,

And so escape the keen edge of resentment.

31

RODRIGUE.   No, the beloved one I have dared to
20   injure
Cannot demand my life too eagerly,
And if I can increase her wrath, I'll win
More speedy death thereby, and so avoid
A thousand deaths of anguish at my crime.
    ELVIRE.   All bathed in tears, Chimene is at the
25   palace.
When she returns, 'twill be with proper escort.
Rodrigue, I beg you, fly and end my fear;
If you were seen here, and some slanderous tongue
Should speak abroad that fair Chimene did harbour
30 Her father's murderer, 'twould add woe to misery.
She'll soon be here. Ay me, I see her come;
Be quick, and hide yourself, for honor's sake.

SCENE II

[*Enter* CHIMENE *and* DON SANCHE]

    SANCHE.   Yes, Madam, bloody deeds ask bloody
        vengeance.
Yours is just anger, these are righteous tears,
I speak thus not to console or gentle you,
But to beseech you, should you deem me worthy,
5 To let my sword destroy the guilty one,
Command my love to seek your father's vengeance;
In serving you, my strength will be redoubled.
    CHIMENE.   O wretched plight!
    SANCHE.   Pray you, accept my service.
    CHIMENE.   Nay, 'twould offend the King, who
        promised justice.
    SANCHE.   You know with what a sluggish step
10   she moves,
How oft her tardy hand leaves crime unpunished.

Her slow and fumbling course brings only tears.
Suffer a knight to take arms and avenge you.
There lies the path most sure and swift to justice.
    CHIMENE. 'Twill be my last resort; if I come
        to it   15
And my unhappy fate still stirs your pity,
Then do I give you leave to be my champion.
    SANCHE. This is the joy whereon my heart was
        bent;
Now I am free to hope, I go content.   [*Exit*]

SCENE III

    CHIMENE. Now, I am free at last, and unre-
        strained,
I can my soul unburden and lay bare
The sharpened edge of grief, heave gusty sighs,
Open my heart wherein such sadness lies.
My father's dead, Elvire, and the first blade   5
Rodrigue had ever wielded cut him down.
Weep, weep, my eyes, dissolve yourselves in tears!
One precious part of life's entombed the other,
And by that cursed blow, makes me avenge
The part I've lost on that which still remains.   10
    ELVIRE. Madam, be calm.
    CHIMENE.   Be calm, she says, be calm!
When the weight of such misfortune bears me
        down!
Yet how can I this horrid grief allay,
If I cannot hate the guilty hand that slew him?
If I avenge a crime, loving the criminal,   15
What can I hope for but eternal torment?
    ELVIRE. He slew your father, yet you love him
        still?

CHIMENE. Love him, Elvire? I worship him, and passion
Has taken arms against my righteous wrath.
20 My lover is my enemy. In my heart
The horrid duel between them still goes on.
Rodrigue attacks my father, drives him back,
A moment yields, fights back, now strong, now feeble,
He wins awhile, but in this fiery combat
25 Of love and hate, he ne'er can win my soul,
Despite the power of love, I shall not waver,
But go, unfaltering, where honor leads me.
Rodrigue is dear to me, his love afflicts me,
Yet I, a daughter, see my father dead.
30 ELVIRE. You would ask his life?
    CHIMENE.   Alas! How cruel the thought!
How cruel the prosecution I am forced to!
I must demand his life, yet fear to take it;
If he dies, I shall die, yet I must slay him!
    ELVIRE. Madam, you must forego so dark a plan,
35 Nor set upon yourself so stern a task.
    CHIMENE. My father dies, and almost in my arms,
His blood cries vengeance and I shall not hear!
My heart shall yield itself to shameful charms,
And I shall owe him naught but empty tears!
40 Shall I then offer the hand of wily passion,
To still a mouth that cries aloud for justice?
    ELVIRE. Believe me, Madam, the world would soon forgive you
If you should feel less anger, when you love
The very man whose life you are forced to take.

You have done enough, you have told the King
    your grievance;   45
Cling not so fiercely to this strange resolve.
    CHIMENE.   My honor's at stake and honor tells
    me vengeance.
Love may deceive us with its sweet desires,
But noble souls find such excuses shameful.
    ELVIRE.   But if you love Rodrigue, how can you
    hate him?   50
    CHIMENE.   I cannot.
    ELVIRE.   Then, what do you plan to do?
    CHIMENE.   To guard my honor, and my tears to
    dry:
Pursue him, slay him, then in sorrow, die.

SCENE IV

[*Enter* DON RODRIGUE]

    RODRIGUE.   Well, then, you need not trouble to
    pursue me;
Assure yourself of honor and my life.
    CHIMENE.   Elvire, where are we? Who is this I
    see?
Rodrigue here, in my house? Rodrigue before me?
    RODRIGUE.   Spare me not, but taste the sweetness
    of my death   5
And your revenge, for I shall not resist.
    CHIMENE.   Alas!
    RODRIGUE.   Hear me.
    CHIMENE.   I die.
    RODRIGUE.   A moment, heed.
    CHIMENE.   Go, leave me to die.
    RODRIGUE.   I beg you, hear me;
Then you may make your answer with this sword.

CHIMENE.   That sword, still reddened with my
10   father's blood?
    RODRIGUE.   Chimene.
    CHIMENE.   Remove that hateful sight, it cries
Aloud against your crime, against your life.
    RODRIGUE.   Look on it rather to excite your hate,
Increase your anger, hasten thus my death.
15   CHIMENE.   My blood has stained it.
    RODRIGUE.   Plunge it into mine.
Then will you wipe away the stain on yours.
    CHIMENE.   How cruel a day that thus can kill us
      both;
He by its thrust, his daughter by its sight;
Take it from hence, I cannot bear to see it.
20 You bid me listen, yet you strike me dead!
              [RODRIGUE *puts up the sword*]
    RODRIGUE.   I'll do your bidding, yet still do I
     desire
To end my wretched life, at your dear hand.
But this you must not ask, that I renounce
My worthy act in cowardly repentance.
25 The fatal outcome of too swift an anger
Disgraced my father, covered me with shame.
You know how a blow affects a man of courage.
I took that blow upon me, sought its author,
And finding him, restored my father's honor.
30 Were it to do again, then I would do it.
'Tis true, against my father and my honor,
My love fought hard and long; O wondrous power,
That I could hesitate to take my vengeance.
When such an offense had touched me, I was
     bound
35 To make you hate me, or to suffer insult,
And so I thought my hand too swift, too eager,

Accused myself of too much violence;
And thus your beauty would have won the day,
But for the thought, still stronger than your charms,
That no man, once dishonored, could deserve you. 40
That though I had a place within your heart,
'Twas for the noble soul, and not the coward.
So to obey my love, to heed its voice,
Would be unworthy, and disgrace your choice.
I tell you once again, though the telling hurts me, 45
And I shall say it to my dying breath;
I did you wrong, yet this wrong had to be,
To cleanse my name, and deserve well of you.
Now honor's satisfied, my father avenged,
'Tis you I come to offer satisfaction. 50
I have come here to offer you my life.
What I have owed, is paid; I owe you this:
Your father, slain, set you in arms against me,
And I would not deprive you of your victim.
So then, fear not, but to this blood outpoured, 55
Sacrifice him who glories to have shed it.
　CHIMENE.　Rodrigue, 'tis true I am your enemy,
Yet cannot blame you when you spurn disgrace.
Know that however loud I weep and wail,
'Tis not in accusation, but in sorrow. 60
I know what pride demands when so outraged,
I know the swift retort of valiant hearts;
You have done your duty as a brave man must,
But doing so, alas, you taught me mine.
Your deadly valor serves me as example, 65
You have avenged your father, saved your honor,
And I must do as much, my honor save,
My father still avenge. But, O despair,
'Tis you who took him off; were it another,
Or some misfortune that had ta'en my father, 70

The sight of you had meant my soul's relief.
When your dear hand had wiped away my tears,
That would have been the most potent charm of all.
But now he's gone, and I must ask your life.
75 Honor demands that thus I still my love,
And horrid duty, like an overseer,
Drives me to work your ruin and my own.
Yet this you must not ask, that I renounce
For love of you, my claim that you be punished.
80 Whate'er in your behalf love pleads with me,
My strength of purpose now must equal yours.
By this your crime you have deserved my love,
So to deserve your love, I seek your death.
    RODRIGUE.   Tarry no more then, do as honor bids
       you,
85 My head must fall, I kneel at last before you,
Come, sacrifice me to this noble cause,
The blow will be sweet to me, and sweet your
       sentence.
After my crime, to wait for tardy justice,
Would put off glory quite as long as death;
90 I shall die happy by so fair a hand.
    CHIMENE.   Go to, I am the plaintiff, not the
       headsman.
Though you offer your life, could it be mine to
       take?
I must demand it, as you must defend it.
Another hand must carry out the sentence;
95 I am your prosecutor, not your slayer.
    RODRIGUE.   Whate'er in my behalf love pleads
       with you,
Your strength of purpose now must equal mine.
This equal power, Chimene, you'll ne'er attain

If you take other arms to avenge your father.
My hand alone avenged my father's shame;   100
Your hand alone should vengeance take on me.
   CHIMENE.   How cruelly you hammer on this
      theme!
Alone, you took your vengeance; so shall I.
Faithful to your example I'll not suffer
That you should share my glory; my own courage, 105
My father, honor, these shall owe you nothing,
Be it your love or your despair that prompts you.
   RODRIGUE.   O stubborn sense of honor, shall I
      never,
Whate'er I do, obtain this final mercy?
In the name of love, in the name of your dead fa-
      ther,   110
Kill me for vengeance, or at least for pity.
For me, your wretched love, 'twere far more easy,
To die at your hand than live to bear your hate.
   CHIMENE.   I do not hate you.
   RODRIGUE.   Yet you should.
   CHIMENE.   I cannot.
   RODRIGUE.   Do you not then fear blame, or the
      tongue of scandal?   115
For when men learn my crime, and know your love
Has still endured, what tales will malice tell!
Enforce their silence then, delay no more,
Strike me down, and so preserve your name.
   CHIMENE.   It will shine brighter if I spare your
      life.   120
Then let the voice of blackest envy cry
To highest heaven my glory and my sorrow,
Because I loved and yet I sought your end.
Go then, take from my presence and my tears

125 What I must slay, loving it all the while.
Pray, as you go, take darkness for your mantle.
If you are seen to leave, my name's at stake,
For now the only chance for slanderous tongues
Is knowing I allowed your presence here.
130 Give them no weapon to attack my virtue.
    RODRIGUE. Rather, I'd die!
    CHIMENE.   Be gone.
    RODRIGUE.   What will you do?
    CHIMENE. E'en though my love does make my
        anger waver,
I shall seek vengeance worthy of my father.
Yet spite of duty's stern commands, I pray
135 I shall accomplish nothing.
    RODRIGUE.   O wondrous love!
    CHIMENE. O heavy pain!
    RODRIGUE.   What tears our fathers cost us!
    CHIMENE. Who could believe, Rodrigue?
    RODRIGUE.   Or who foretell?
    CHIMENE. Our happiness, so near, should swiftly
        vanish?
    RODRIGUE. Our hope, nearing the harbor, un-
        foreseen,
140 Should break and founder in the sudden storm?
    CHIMENE. Woe, mortal woe!
    RODRIGUE.   Alas, we weep in vain!
    CHIMENE. Once more, I pray you, go, I must
        not listen.
    RODRIGUE. I shall drag out what's left to me of
        life,
Till your avenging hand shall cut its thread.
    CHIMENE. If I obtain that end, my word I
145   pledge:
I shall not breathe a moment after you.

Farewell; go you now, and pray you, go unseen.
    ELVIRE.   Madam, whate'er misfortunes Heaven
        sends us . . .
    CHIMENE.   Leave me in peace, I beg you; leave
        me to sigh,
To cover myself in darkness and to cry.   [*Exeunt*] 150

SCENE V

[*Enter* DON DIEGUE, *alone*]

    DON DIEGUE.   Man never tastes a perfect hap-
        piness,
His greatest joys are ever tinged with sadness.
Amidst each great success some mote of care
Sullies the radiant beam of pure contentment.
My bliss is shadowed by the fear of woe,   5
My heart o'erflows and yet I shake with terror;
The enemy who disgraced me now lies dead,
And now I cannot find my brave avenger.
In vain I seek him, wandering through the city,
Broken in strength and weary, I have spent   10
What little vigor's left me searching for him.
Each minute, in the dark, now here, now there,
My arms embrace him, yet hold empty air.
And thus deceived by shadows and dread thoughts,
My fear increases as the moments pass,   15
I see no trace to tell me he has fled.
I fear the dead Count's friends, his entourage;
Their number frightens me, confounds my brain,
Rodrigue is dead or else he lives in prison.
Just Heavens! Does another vision trick me,   20
Or do I see before me my life's hope?
'Tis he, I doubt no more, I fear no more,
My prayers are granted, and my cares are o'er.

Scene VI

[*Enter* Don Rodrigue]

Don Diegue. Rodrigue! Heaven at last has
    heard my prayers!
Rodrigue. Alas!
Don Diegue. Come not with sighs to mar my
    joy,
O let me take my breath, the more to praise you.
My valor has no cause to disavow you,
5 For you have matched it, and your daring deeds
Revive again the heroes of our race.
You are their true descendant and my offspring.
Your sword's first thrust has equaled all my own,
Your youth with glorious ardor set aflame,
10 Threatens by this great deed my own renown.
O strength of my old age, and crowning joy,
Touch these white hairs whose honor you've re-
    stored;
Come, kiss this cheek whereon the foul blow fell,
Whose mark you have effacèd by your courage.
    Rodrigue. This honor was your due, I could do
15   no less.
Sprung from your loins, reared by your loving care,
'Tis my good fortune to have served you well,
And to have pleased the author of my days
In my first contest. Yet do not be jealous,
20 Now I have done your bidding, if my cries,
My deep despair, burst forth and know no check.
Too long your soothing words have quelled my
    anguish.
That I have served you I shall ne'er regret,
But let me find again what my deed has lost.

My arm, avenging you, struck down my love,   25
And by this glorious blow my heart reft from me.
Say nothing more, for you I have abandoned
All that I held most dear; my debt is paid.
  DON DIEGUE. Count not so cheap the spoils of
          victory:
I gave you life, you gave me back my honor.   30
And since I hold honor dearer far than life,
So do I owe you far more in return.
Let your stout heart be firm; we've but one honor;
And there are many mistresses to choose from.
Love is sweet dalliance, honor sternest duty.   35
  RODRIGUE.   What words are these?
  DON DIEGUE.   Such words as you must hear.
  RODRIGUE.   Thus do I pay the price of love be-
          trayed!
You dare suggest a shameful breath of faith!
The faithless lover and the craven warrior
Are one in infamy; therefore, do not blame me   40
If I am faithful, let me both be valiant,
And true to love. Such bonds are not lightly broken.
Though I despair, I have sworn constancy,
I cannot win, nor yet forsake Chimene,
So I'll seek death, the sooner to end my pain.   45
  DON DIEGUE. This is no time to talk of seeking
          death;
Your prince, your country, need your stalwart arm.
The ships we feared have sailed into the river.
They plan to take the town and sack the region.
The Moors are upon us, and the evening tide   50
In an hour will softly bear them to our walls.
Disorder reigns in the court, and the frantic mob
Run shouting and wailing through the city streets.
In this misfortune, fortune favored me:

55 Five hundred friends had gathered at my home;
   Spurred by righteous zeal they'd come to avenge
      me.
   Your arm forestalled them; now their bravery,
   For this delay, shall strike the Moor more fiercely.
   Your place is at their head, you shall command
60 These noble troops 'gainst our old enemy.
   If you must die, seek there a worthy death;
   Seize now the chance; make the King owe his safety
   To your noble death or to your victory;
   Return if you can, wearing the victor's palms.
65 Restrict no more your triumphs to mere vengeance;
   Carry them farther, and by valiant strokes
   Force the King to pardon and Chimene to silence.
   For if you love her, then the surest path
   Back to her heart, is to return a conqueror.
70 But time's too dear to waste in idle words;
   My talk detains you, yet I would speed you on.
   Away to battle; show the King, your lord,
   What he lost in the Count, in you is now restored.

Act IV

❧

SCENE I

[Enter CHIMENE *and* ELVIRE*]*

CHIMENE. This is no rumor? You are sure,
    Elvire?

ELVIRE. The people sing his exploits with one
    voice,

Praising their youthful hero to the skies.

The Moors appeared before him to their shame,

Swift was their landing, swifter still their flight.   5

Three hours of combat brought as his reward,

A total victory, and two kings our prisoners.

CHIMENE. 'Tis Don Rodrigue who worked these
    miracles?

ELVIRE. This royal prize we owe to his en-
    deavors,

He conquered them; to him did they surrender.   10

CHIMENE. Pray, who has brought you these
    amazing tidings?

ELVIRE. The grateful populace, who name him
    author

Of all their joys, their country's benefactor,

Our guardian angel, who has made us free.

CHIMENE. The King, what thinks he of such
    valiant deeds?   15

ELVIRE. Rodrigue has not yet dared appear be-
    fore him,

Albeit his beaming father has presented

The royal prisoners to his royal master,
And in their conqueror's name, demands his par-
    don,
20 And speedy audience, as recompense
To one who saved his kingdom.
    CHIMENE.   Is he wounded?
    ELVIRE. I know not. But you turn pale! Be
    calm, I pray you.
    CHIMENE. Let me not calm my anger, 'tis too
    weak,
Calming may quench it. Ah, must I forget
25 Through so much thought of him my solemn bond?
He's vaunted, praised, and my poor heart exults.
My honor's mute, my sense of duty feebled;
Silence, O love; anger, bestir yourself:
Two kings he's taken, but he killed my father.
30 These woeful trappings cry aloud my sorrow,
'Tis he who decked me in them, by his prowess.
Howe'er men praise his staunch and noble heart,
Here every object shouts his crime to Heaven.
Ye that lend fuel to my smouldering wrath,
35 Ye crepes and veils that costume the bereaved,
Strengthen my wavering honor, smother passion,
And when my love becomes too powerful,
Recall my spirit to its stern decision,
Fear not to match yourselves against a hero.
    ELVIRE. Pray you, restrain your grief; the Prin-
40   cess comes.

SCENE II

[Enter the INFANTA *and* LEONOR]

    INFANTA. I come not to console your pain,
    Chimene,

But rather my sighs to mingle with your tears.

  CHIMENE. Nay, Madam, join your plaudits to
      the crowd's;

Embrace the fortune Heaven has brought to all,

No one but me has any right to weep. 5

The perils he has saved us from, his valor,

Whereby the public weal's preserved, can suffer

No lamentations but my own. The King,

The realm, owe him their safety, but to me,

The power of his arms is merely deadly. 10

  INFANTA. 'Tis true, Chimene, he has done mira-
      cles.

  CHIMENE. I have already heard the dire report,

And I have heard him everywhere proclaimed,

As brave in war as he's distrest in love.

  INFANTA. But why should this report seem so
      disastrous? 15

This son of Mars they praise was once your lover,

Your heart was his, he lived beneath your sway;

To vaunt his power does honor to your choice.

  CHIMENE. 'Tis just that others praise him, but
      to me,

Such high esteem is torture, and to hear 20

Men value him shows me what I have lost.

Ah, cruel distress that wracks a lover's heart!

The more I know his worth, the more I love him,

And yet my duty ever shall prevail,

And seek his death despite the pangs of love. 25

  INFANTA. This strong resolve could yesterday
      be praised.

Your noble firmness moved the court to tears

Of pity and admiration. But would you heed

A faithful friend's advice?

  CHIMENE.   I would be base

30 Did I not heed you.
     INFANTA.   Hear me then, Chimene.
What then was just, no more is so today;
Rodrigue is now the country's sole support,
The love and hope of an adoring people,
Castille's firm bastion, terror of the Moor.
35 The King himself supports the general view,
That in Rodrigue his father lives again.
In a word, Chimene, if you still seek his death,
You seek the public ruin. Nay what folly,
To offer up one's country to its foes,
40 So to avenge a father. Are we criminals
That we should be pursued for another's crime?
You shall not, after all, be forced to marry
One whom your father's death forced you to hate.
I hope myself that I may quell your passion;
45 Deprive him of your love, grant us his life.
     CHIMENE. Alas! I have no right to grant this
         boon;
The charge that spurs me knows no limitation.
Despite my love, despite the royal acclaim,
Despite the crowd's applause, the valiant band
50 That swears devotion to him, I must spread
A deadly cypress branch upon his laurels.
     INFANTA. These would be noble words, if a
         father's vengeance
Were all at stake, but for the public good,
'Twere nobler far to sacrifice your claims.
55 To still the voice of love is proof enough
Of honor to your father, and for his slayer
'Tis cruel punishment. Come, I beseech you,
Let the good of the realm impose this course upon
         you.
For what think you the King will grant you now?

CHIMENE.   He may refuse me, I cannot be si-
    lent.   60
INFANTA.   Think well, Chimene, what you're
    about to do.
Adieu, I leave you to reflect alone.
CHIMENE.   My father's dead; the choice is not
    my own.   [*Exeunt*]

SCENE III

[*Enter* DON FERNAND, DON DIEGUE, DON ARIAS,
    DON RODRIGUE, *and* DON SANCHE]

DON FERNAND [*To* RODRIGUE].   Most noble scion
    of a glorious race,
One that was e'er the pride of all Castille,
Your deed has equaled the most mighty feats
Your valiant ancestors performed for Spain.
To give you just reward outstrips my power,   5
Your merit is too great. The realm delivered
From its fierce enemy, my scepter saved,
The Moors defeated e'er I could give the signal
That they should be repulsed! Such exploits
Can never find a worthy recompense.   10
But let the kings, your captives, grant you honor,
Since in my presence they have named you "Cid,"
Which in their tongue does mean a mighty lord,
Hencefore you shall be *Cid*, and let this name
Strike terror in the heart of all Grenada,   15
And set Toledo trembling. This brave title
Shall show to all my subjects what I owe you,
And be a warrant of my love for you.
    DON RODRIGUE.   Sire, shame me not by placing
        too much value
On services so slight. I blush to hear   20

Praise from so great a king for deeds so small.
Yes, I am too much honored, for I owe
My life's blood and the very air I breathe
To keep your realm secure; and should I lose them
25 In such a cause, I would but do my duty.
    DON FERNAND.   But all who do their duty in my
        service,
Bring not such mighty courage to the doing;
'Tis only valor far beyond most men
Can work such proud successes. Grant us then
30 The right to praise you, and relate to us,
In full detail the story of your triumph.
    DON RODRIGUE.   Well, Sire, you knew that in
        this pressing danger,
That sent a chill of horror through the city,
A group of friends, assembled at our home,
35 Sought to appeal to my heart in its upheaval . . .
But Sire, excuse my boldness, for I acted,
Lacking your royal warrant, yet the peril
Was close upon us, and our force was ready.
To come to the court I would have risked my life,
40 And if I had to die, 'twere better far
To offer up my life in your defense.
    DON FERNAND.   I now forgive your fierce and
        bloody vengeance;
The land you have preserved pleads your defense.
Chimene henceforth shall ask your life in vain,
45 And I shall grant her pleas naught but my pity.
Enough, say on.
    DON RODRIGUE.   Forward I led the troops;
On every forehead shone a firm assurance.
We were five hundred, but our ranks soon swelled,
Till, when we reached the port, we were three
        thousand,

Such was the courage our expressions stirred   50
In the most frightened watchers. No sooner there,
Two thirds of our men I hid in boats that lay there.
The rest, whose numbers grew with every hour,
Now cluster 'round me, check their fiery spirits,
Crouch close to earth, without a breath of sound; 55
And so they pass most of this lovely night.
The guard, on my instructions, does the same,
And keeping hidden, aids my stratagem.
I boldly claim it is by royal command
I take this course, and summon all to follow.   60
The light that dimly from the stars does fall,
At last, on the rising tide, shows thirty sails;
The waters surge beneath them, and together,
The Moors and the sea are borne into the port.
We let them pass; they find all wrapped in silence. 65
No soldiers guard the port or city walls.
Deceived by this great stillness, they are sure
They have surprised us, and with tranquil hearts,
They dock, cast anchor, swiftly disembark,
And give themselves into our waiting hands.   70
We leap to our feet, and in one mighty voice,
Hurl to the skies our joyful battle cry.
Our men in the ships send back an answering
          shout,
They show their arms, the Moors fall in confusion;
Though scarcely disembarked, they're seized with
          terror,   75
And e'er the fight begins, take all for lost.
They came to pillage, and found war instead;
On land, on water do we hurl them back,
E'er they can form their ranks again, we shed
Rivers of Moorish blood. But 'tis not long   80
Before their princes rally the desperate band;

The shame of death without a struggle steels them,
Mends their disorder, and restores their strength.
No more in terror, but with new-born courage,
85 They turn their alien blades against our ranks,
Their blood and ours soon flow in horrid mixture,
The land, the river, and the fleet and port,
Are fields of bloody havoc, death triumphant.
Oh, what noble deeds, what valiant exploits,
90 Thus cloaked in dark, will ne'er be known to fame.
Each fighter, the sole witness of his blows,
Forever ignorant of the tide of fate!
On every side I cheered our fighters on;
Urged one group forward, gave support to others,
95 Sent in our reinforcements in their turn,
And till the dawn, I could not know the outcome.
But at last, its light shows us our victory,
The Moor, seeing his loss, loses his courage;
Sighting new troops that come to reinforce us,
100 His urge to conquer bows to the fear of death.
They rush to their vessels, screaming as they go;
Cut off the cables, fall back in disorder,
With no thought for their kings, their fears too
    great.
The tide that brought them bears them out to sea.
105 Meantime the kings with a handful of their men
Despite their wounds fight valiantly against us,
Sell their lives dearly, and to all my pleas
That they surrender, brandish scimitars.
But when they see their last few soldiers fallen,
110 Knowing that now resistance would be vain,
They call for our chief, and when I name myself,
Lay down their arms. I sent both here together.
Thus, lacking combatants, the combat ended.
And so it was, Sire, striving e'er to serve you . . .

[*Enter* DON ALONSE]

DON ALONSE.   Sire, 'tis Chimene who comes to
    sue for justice.   115
DON FERNAND.   This is bad news. How tiresome
    are our duties!
[*To* RODRIGUE]
Get you gone; I would not have her see you here.
This is a sorry thanks, to be dismissed!
But e'er you go, come, let your king embrace you.
              [*They embrace; exit* RODRIGUE]
DON DIEGUE.   Chimene pursues him, but would
    rather save him.   120
DON FERNAND.   I've heard she still does love
    him. I would try her;
Put on a mournful look.

SCENE IV

[*Enter* CHIMENE]

          At last, Chimene,
Success has crowned your efforts; Don Rodrigue,
Though he has triumphed o'er our enemy,
Died from his wounds just now, before our eyes.
Give thanks to Heaven, that it has avenged you.
[*To* DON DIEGUE, *aside*]
See how she changes color at the news.   5
DON DIEGUE.   But look, she swoons, and by this
    faintness shows,
The power of deepest love; thus is betrayed
By sorrow's signs, the secret of her soul.
You can no longer doubt her love is real.
CHIMENE.   Rodrigue is dead, you say?   10
DON FERNAND.   No, no, he lives,

And loves you with a never-changing passion.
End then, the grief this false report has caused you.
>CHIMENE.   We swoon, my lord, from joy as well
>   as grief,
Excess of pleasure weakens our control,
15 And such surprise can overcome the senses.
>DON FERNAND.   You ask us to believe the impos-
>   sible?
Chimene, your grief was all too evident.
>CHIMENE.   Well then, sire, call it the climax to
>   misfortune,
Declare my fainting an effect of grief.
20 'Twas a just anger that o'erwhelmed me so;
His death had meant I could no longer seek it.
And if he dies from wounds incurred in battle,
My vengeance is no more, my plans awry.
So glorious an end would be unjust;
25 I claim his death, but not so fair a leaving;
Not on the field of honor, sanctified,
But on a scaffold, punished for his crime.
Let his name be published, not with glorious fan-
>   fare,
But stained, disgraced, of shameful memory.
30 To die for fatherland is no sad fate;
So fair a death grants immortality.
His victory pleases me, and rightly so:
It saves the realm, and yields me up my victim.
Ennobled by his feats, great among warriors,
His head crowned, not with flowers, but laurels
35   proud,
Fit for a sacrifice to my father's spirit.
Alas! What foolish hopes excite my brain!
Rodrigue has naught to fear from such as I,

Whose tears men scorn; enjoying your protection,
In all the empire he's above the law. 40
In me he has vanquished still another foe,
He has drowned justice in his enemies' gore,
Tramples the laws beneath his chariot wheels,
Drags us behind him, in his proud procession,
Beside the captive kings, another prisoner. 45
    DON FERNAND. Soft you, my daughter, here's too
        great a violence,
Dealing justice, one must weigh both sides.
Your father was killed, yet he was the aggressor;
Justice alone ordained that I be lenient.
Before accusing me of too much laxness, 50
Look into your heart, Rodrigue is ruler there,
And secretly your love gives thanks to me,
That my indulgence so preserves your lover.
    CHIMENE. Preserves my lover! Rather say my
        foe,
Author of all my woes, my father's slayer. 55
You think my wish for vengeance is so weak,
That you oblige me when you will not hear me.
Since you refuse, Sire, to be moved by tears,
Grant me permission to take arms against him.
'Twas by that means he did me grievous harm, 60
And by that means I must avenge this wrong.
I ask of all your knights to take his life;
Whoever conquers him, I'll gladly wed.
Sire, let them fight, and when the contest's over,
I'll wed the victor, if it be not Rodrigue. 65
Let this be published as a royal decree.
    DON FERNAND. This ancient custom, here so
        long established,
Under the guise of punishing misdeeds,

Has bled the state of its stoutest fighting men.
70 And oft indeed the duel's dread result
Favors the guilty and destroys the guiltless.
Rodrigue I do exempt, he is too precious
To bear the brunt of a capricious fate.
Whate'er the crime this noble soul has done,
75 The Moors he routed bore away his guilt.
    CHIMENE.   What, Sire! for him alone o'erthrow the law
That all the court so often has observed?
What will the people think, and envy say
If he preserve his life by your protection,
80 And so excuse his failure to appear
Where men of honor seek a glorious death?
Such favors would besmirch his reputation;
Let him unblushing taste the fruits of victory.
The Count was overbold; he punished him,
'Twas a brave man's deed, and brave he should
85   remain.
    DON FERNAND.   Since you desire it, let it then be done.
But for every one he slays, a thousand more
Would take his place; the prize Chimene has promised
Would make of all my knights his enemies,
90 'Twould be unjust that he should fight them all.
A single contest must suffice, Chimene.
Choose well your champion, for when they have fought,
The die is cast; I shall grant nothing more.
    DON DIEGUE.   Sire, this but makes excuse for those who fear
95 To meet him. Pray you, leave an open field,

For none will enter it, knowing his prowess.
Who so foolhardy as to match with him?
Who would risk all 'gainst such an adversary,
Who is so brave, or rather, so imprudent?

    DON SANCHE.   Open the field, here is your chal-
        lenger.   100

I shall imprudent be, or rather, brave.
Madam, grant me this boon, for you have promised
To grant my wish to serve as your defender.

    DON FERNAND.   Chimene, do you accept this
        champion?

    CHIMENE.   Sire, I have promised it.   105

    DON FERNAND.   They fight tomorrow.

    DON DIEGUE.   Nay, sire, the combat must not be
        delayed,

The brave in heart stand always at the ready.

    DON FERNAND.   To fight again so soon after the
        battle?

    DON DIEGUE.   Rodrigue had rest enough in tell-
        ing it.

    DON FERNAND.   At least he must repose an hour
        or two.   110

And lest this duel should set a precedent,
To show to all the loathing that I feel
For such a bloody business, neither I
Nor any of my court shall witness it.
[*To* DON ARIAS]
You shall be sole judge of the combatants.   115
Take care that they observe the code of honor,
And when the fighting's done, bring me the victor.
Whoe'er he be, his prize shall be the same:
I shall myself present him to Chimene;
For his reward, he shall receive her hand.   120

CHIMENE.   What, Sire? This cruel sentence shall
    be mine?
  DON FERNAND.   You balk at it, but deep within,
    your love
Will ne'er complain if the victor be Rodrigue.
Cease then to murmur, and my will abide,
125 Whoever wins shall have Chimene for bride.

Act V

[Enter Rodrigue *and* Chimene*]*

Chimene.   What! In the light of day! Rodrigue
    before me!
You dare too much; leave, e'er you stain my honor.
    Rodrigue.   Madam, my death is near, and I have
    come
To say a last farewell e'er the blow falls;
The deathless love that holds me in your sway   5
Must offer up my life upon your altar.
    Chimene.   Your death is near!
    Rodrigue.   The happy hour approaches
When I shall pay with life for your displeasure.
    Chimene.   Your death is near! Don Sanche is to
    be feared,
And so dismays a heart as yet unconquered?   10
What has so weakened you, what gives him
    strength?
Rodrigue's about to fight, and waits for death?
He did not fear my father, or the Moors,
Yet he despairs with Sanche his adversary!
And thus, in greatest need, your courage fails!   15
    Rodrigue.   I seek my death, and not the strife of
    combat;
Loving you as I do, can I desire
To save my life, when you demand my death?
My courage undismayed, yet shrinks to fight
So to preserve that which displeases you.   20

The night that's past would have been mortal to me,
Had I been fighting for my cause alone.
But for a king, his people, and his realm,
'Twere cowardice to ill defend oneself..

25 Noble am I, yet I do not hate life
Enough to lose it by an act of treason.
Now that I fight for no one but myself,
You claim my death, and I accept your edict.
In anger you have chosen another's hand

30 To strike the blow—alas, I could not hope
To die by yours. I shall make no defense.
Greater respect than this I owe your champion.
I shall rejoice knowing his blows are yours;
Since 'tis your honor that his blade defends,

35 I'll meet his challenge with unguarded breast,
Adoring by his hand your own that slays me.
    CHIMENE.   If the just violence of this wretched
        bond
That makes of me your helpless prosecutor,
Inflicts so harsh a law upon your love

40 That you'll defenseless stand against my champion,
Remember, in your blindness, that your honor
As well as life's at stake; and should you die,
However great has been your fame in life,
The world will say that you have died defeated.

45 Your honor's dearer far than I am dear,
Since for its sake you spilled my father's blood,
Renounced your passion and your dearest hope
Of my possession. Yet do you not esteem it,
For unresisting, you would be defeated.

50 What whim so undermines your resolution?
Whence has it flown, or why was it so firm?
Are you great-hearted only when it wrongs me?
And since I can no longer be offended,

Have you lost all courage? Why attack my father
Most cruelly slay him, then accept defeat?   55
Nay, seek not death, and let me still pursue you,
Though you hate life, at least defend your honor.
  RODRIGUE. The Count lies slain, the Moorish
    foe's defeated;
Must I still other proofs of glory find?
My honor need not deign to plead its cause,   60
Men know there's naught my courage will not dare.
They know my valor, and that under Heaven,
Nothing I cherish if it be not honor.
Nay, in this fight, I say, Rodrigue may fall,
And never be accused of lacking courage,   65
Nor ever seem defeated, own no victor,
Men will say only, "He adored Chimene,
He could not live, knowing he'd earned her hatred;
Thus did he suffer the cruel will of fate
That forced his mistress to demand his death.   70
She asked his life, and to this noble spirit,
Refusing her this boon were criminal.
He lost his love to keep his honor fair;
To keep her honor fair, he lost his life,
Preferring still, whatever hopes he cherished,   75
His honor to Chimene, Chimene to his life."
So in this conflict, shall my death apply
No stain, but rather luster, to my glory,
And by my willing death, proclaim your honor,
That no one's life but mine could e'er assuage it. 80
  CHIMENE. Since life and honor have so little
    power
To check this mortal rush, then hear my plea:
If ever, dear Rodrigue, I loved you well,
Defend yourself to save me from Don Sanche.
Fight to preserve me from an odious fate,   85

That would deliver me to one I hate.
Must I say more? Go, see to your defense.
Make me renounce my duty; silence me,
And if you love me still, return the victor,
90 For you do battle with Chimene as prize.
Farewell. I blush with shame; these words escaped
        me.   [*Exit*]
    RODRIGUE.   Where now is any foe I cannot slay!
Come on, you Navarrese, Castilians, Moors!
And all the bravest warriors of Spain!
95 Unite together, make yourselves an army,
To fight against a man inspired as I am.
Against so sweet a hope, your mightiest do;
E'en in your thousands, you shall be too few.

                                            [*Exit*]

SCENE II

[*Enter the* INFANTA, *alone*]

Then must I heed thee still, O noble source,
        That love a crime does make?
Or must I heed thee, love, whose gentle force
Tells me such tyrant laws are fit to break?
5   Unhappy princess, take
        One or the other course:
Rodrigue, your valor merits my embrace:
Valorous you are, yet not of royal race.

Fate most unkind, that sternly keeps apart
10   My fame, my hopes most high!
Why must my passion suffer grievous hurt
For choosing one who strove so mightily?
        For many a gloomy sigh
        I must prepare my heart,

Unless this torment I can end forever, 15
And either quell the love, or take the lover!

Enough of scruples, common sense must frown,
    When I so hesitate;
Though princesses may marry kings alone,
Rodrigue, with honor I would be your mate. 20
    Did you not two kings defeat?
    How then do you lack a crown?
The mighty name of Cid does clearly prove
You fit to rule a princess and her love.

Yes, he is worthy, but he loves Chimene: 25
    I suffer that I willed it so.
A father's death did scarcely intervene,
And her pursuit of him is strangely slow.
    Nothing shall come, I know
    Of his crime, or my pain, 30
Since fate permits, the worse to punish me,
That these two enemies should lovers be.

SCENE III

[*Enter* LEONOR]

    INFANTA. Where go you, Leonor?
    LEONOR.   I come to praise you
For having found at last, peace and repose.
    INFANTA. Repose and peace? How find them in
        my sorrow?
    LEONOR. If love must live on hope, and die
        without it,
Rodrigue no longer can entrance your heart.
You know Chimene has forced him to a duel; 5
Either he dies, or winning, wins her hand.

Whate'er the outcome, you can hope no longer.
    INFANTA. Ah! how wrong you are!
    LEONOR.   How can you hope?
    INFANTA. Ask me instead how I can cease to
    hope.
10 For I know many schemes to bring to naught
The dire conditions under which he fights.
Love, sweet and cruel love, teaches its victims
A thousand wiles to help them to their goal.
    LEONOR. How can you win, when e'en a father
    slain
15 Could not divide them? By her every act
Chimene has shown her motives are not hate.
She asks a trial by combat, and accepts
As champion the first who volunteers;
She does not seek to fight for her some knight
Whose valiant deeds have brought him great re-
20   nown,
No, 'tis Don Sanche she chooses; he is young,
As yet untried; this is his first encounter.
Because of this she does not fear the outcome,
So weak a choice declares to all the world
25 That by this duel she would renounce her duty.
For when Rodrigue has won an easy victory,
She will seem to have done all that her honor asked.
    INFANTA.   Well do I know it, yet my heart adores
This conquering hero, rivaling Chimene.
30 What shall I do, so wretched is my love?
    LEONOR. Ever remember your exalted source.
Heaven decrees a king must be your mate,
And not a subject.
    INFANTA.   Yet my love has changed:
'Tis not Rodrigue, a nobleman, I love,
35 No longer does he bear so mean a title.

The man I love is the doer of great deeds,
The valiant Cid, the conqueror of two kings.
Yet shall I still my heart, not fearing blame,
But lest I bring dissension on their love.
Yes, should they even crown him for my sake,　　40
I would refuse to take what I have given.
Since in this contest he is sure to triumph,
Come, once again we'll give him to Chimene;
And having seen me bare my wounds most deep,
Now shall you see how my resolve I'll keep.　　45
　　　　　　　　　　　　　　　[Exeunt]

Scene IV

[Enter Chimene *and* Elvire*]*

Chimene.　What agony, Elvire, is mine to suffer!
I know not what to hope, all's to be feared.
My every wish is guilty, each desire
No sooner uttered, prompts my swift repentance.
Two rivals I have made contend for me,　　5
The happiest outcome must be full of woe,
And howsoever fate rewards my hope,
My father's unavenged, or my lover slain.
　　Elvire.　Whate'er the outcome you shall be re-
　　　　quited;
Either Rodrigue, or vengeance shall be yours.　　10
However destiny rules, you are assured
Unblemished honor, and a worthy husband.
　　Chimene.　Yes, one I hate, or one who stirs my
　　　　fury!
Rodrigue's assassin, or my father's slayer!
And either hand they offer me in marriage　　15
Stained with the blood of him I held most dear!
My heart rebels whatever the decision,

And I do fear the outcome more than death.
Vengeance and love, away! No more disturb me!
20 You have no charms for me at such a price.
And thou, great Mover of my horrid fate,
Let there be no decision; let it end
With neither man the winner or the loser.
    ELVIRE.   But that would be the cruelest fate of
       all.
25 This duel would be the source of new distress,
If when 'tis done, you still must ask for justice,
Still cry aloud a hatred so profound,
And still demand the death of him you love.
Madam, 'tis better far his victory,
30 Wreathing his brow with laurels, still your voice,
Stifle your sighs, and by the law of combat,
Make you obey your King, and your own desire.
    CHIMENE.   Think you that if he wins I shall
       surrender?
My duty is too strong, my loss too great,
35 Neither the royal command, nor the law of combat
Can rule them. Sanche may fall, but not my pride.
Despite the royal promise I'll raise up
A thousand champions to defend my honor.
    ELVIRE.   Take care, lest Heaven punish your
       wilful pride,
40 And never grant you vengeance. You refuse
The joy that now with honor may be yours?
What more can duty claim, to what aspire?
Can your lover's death restore your father's life?
Is one misfortune not enough? Or would you
45 Loss upon loss, sorrow on sorrow heap?
Fie, fie, such foolish pride will be rewarded:
You are unworthy of your promised love,
And Heaven in its just anger shall destroy him,

Leaving you Sanche as husband.
　　CHIMENE.　　　　　　　　Stay, no more,
Swell not my torment by such prophecies.　　　50
I would, an if I could, escape them both,
But failing this, my hopes are for Rodrigue,
Think not a foolish passion turns me to him,
Yet I'd be Sanche's prize were he defeated,
And fearing this, I pray that he has won.　　　55
But what is this? Alas, all hope is done!

SCENE V

[Enter DON SANCHE, *bearing his sword]*

　　DON SANCHE.　Madam, I am required to bring
　　　　this sword . . .
　　CHIMENE.　Still reeking with the victim's blood!
　　　　For shame,
Villain, how dare you show yourself before me,
When you have ta'en away all I held dear.
Proclaim thyself, my love, fear nothing more!　　　5
My father is avenged, thou need'st not hide!
One fatal thrust my honor has assured,
My soul filled with despair, my love set free!
　　DON SANCHE.　With calmer spirit . . .
　　CHIMENE.　　　　　　Still you speak to me,
O wretched slayer of the man I loved!　　　10
By trickery you slew him; one so brave
Could ne'er succumb to such an adversary.
Ask nothing more of me, this is no service;
You thought to avenge me, yet you took my life.
　　DON SANCHE.　What strange illusion deafens so
　　　　your ears . . .　　　15
　　CHIMENE.　What! Must I hear you boast of how
　　　　you slew him,

Stand patiently the while you paint his fall,
Your valiant deed, and mine, the worst of all?

SCENE VI

[*Enter* DON FERNAND, DON DIEGUE, DON ARIAS, *and*
DON ALONSE]

No longer, Sire, need I conceal from you
What all my guile was helpless to keep hidden.
I loved him, as you knew, but a father slain,
Demanded that I seek a loved one's death.
5 Your Majesty has seen my constancy,
How I made love bow before duty's claim.
But now Rodrigue is dead, and by his death,
His bitter foe becomes his weeping lover.
Thus to my father, I did owe this vengeance;
10 Thus to my love, now I do owe these tears.
Don Sanche destroys me in my own defense,
And I must be the prize of my destroyer!
Ah, Sire, if ever pity moved a king,
Revoke, I pray you, so severe a law;
15 Let him for his reward in this grim triumph
Take all I own, leaving me free to go,
Within a convent's wall to spend my life
In mourning for a father and a lover.
    DON DIEGUE.   Well, Sire, at last she thinks it is
        no crime
20 To openly confess her rightful love.
    DON FERNAND.   Chimene, you are misled, your
        lover lives;
    Don Sanche was vanquished, and has told you false.
    DON SANCHE.   Sire, she was overwrought, and
        all my efforts
    Failed to undeceive her; I had come

To tell her how our combat was resolved.   25
The valiant knight she loves, when he disarmed me,
Spoke thus to me: "Fear not, for I had rather
The victory be in doubt than shed the blood
You risked for my Chimene; but duty calls,
I'll to the King. Go, tell her of our combat,   30
And as the victor's gift, bear her your sword."
Sire, I obeyed, but seeing me still armed,
She thought I was the victor, and her anger
In sudden outbreak did reveal her love;
So great was her distress, she would not hear me. 35
Thus is my heart defeated, yet withal,
'Tis a defeat I like, for it assures
The happy outcome of a perfect love.
  DON FERNAND.   You need not blush, my child, at
        your devotion,
Nor ever seek again to disavow it.   40
Your honor brightly shines, your duty's done,
Your father is avenged, for 'twas his vengeance
To send Rodrigue so often into danger.
You see how Heaven has ruled otherwise,
You have done much for him, for yourself do this: 45
Accept, obedient, to my royal command,
The husband you adore; give him your hand.

SCENE VII

[Enter the INFANTA *and* ELVIRE, *followed by*
        RODRIGUE]

  INFANTA.   Dry your tears, Chimene, and joyously
        receive
From your princess' hand, a noble warrior.
  RODRIGUE.   [*Falling   on   his   knees   before*
        CHIMENE]

Be not offended, Sire, if here before you,
I kneel to her in token of my love.
5 I come not to demand a prize of conquest,
But rather to offer once again my life.
Madam, fear not, for I shall ne'er invoke
The law of combat, or the royal command.
If all that's done's too little for a father,
10 Tell me what I must do to satisfy you.
Must I combat a thousand rivals more,
Extend my exploits to the ends of earth,
Or singly storm a camp, or rout an army,
Outdo in fame heroes of song and story?
15 If any such could wash away my crime,
I shall dare anything, and all achieve.
But should your honor, ever unappeased,
Demand the criminal's life, no longer seek
The whole world's power, but avenge yourself.
20 Your hand alone can conquer the unconquered;
Take then a vengeance none but you can take.
But let my death suffice as punishment,
Let not my memory fade; remember me,
And since my death shall keep your honor bright,
25 Repay me thus, that when you think on me,
You'll say, "Alas, had he not loved me well,
He would be living still."
    CHIMENE.   Rodrigue, arise.
Sire, I have said too much to deny my love.
His many virtues I could ne'er gainsay,
30 And when a king commands, we must obey.
But Sire, despite your edict, can you suffer
This marriage to take place, whate'er my duty?
Have you no doubts? Rodrigue, for his great valor,
Must then receive me as his just reward?
35 And I must be condemned to shame eternal,

My hands all sullied with a father's blood?
  Don Fernand. Often has time made deeds
      legitimate
That once seemed criminal. Rodrigue has won you,
Yet though his valor conquered you today,
If I so soon bestowed on him his prize,   40
I would appear his honor's enemy.
To stay this marriage alters not a law,
Which set no time in giving him your hand.
Take, if you will, a year to dry your tears.
And you, Rodrigue, meantime take up your arms, 45
The Moors you vanquished here upon our shores,
O'erturned their plans, beat back their fierce as-
      saults.
Take now the war into their Moorish realm,
Command my army and lay waste their lands.
Hearing the name of Cid, they'll shake with fear, 50
They've named you Lord, now shall they make you
      king.
In all your mighty deeds keep faith with her,
Strive to return more worthy of her love,
And by your exploits win such great renown,
That she will then be proud to be your bride.   55
  Rodrigue. To win Chimene, to serve my mon-
      arch well,
What mighty labors shall I not accomplish?
Though far away I must endure her absence,
Sire, 'tis enough you give me leave to hope.
  Don Fernand. Place then your hope in strength
      and in my promise.   60
And since already you have won her heart,
She'll not forever to stern honor cling;
Leave all to time, your valor, and your King.

BIBLIOGRAPHY

The standard definitive French edition of Corneille's works is that of Marty-Laveaux, in the series *Les Grands Ecrivains de la France,* 12 volumes (1862-1868)

In French the best work combining biography and criticism is Robert Brasillach's *Pierre Corneille* (Fayard, 1938); there is an excellent study of Cornelian dramaturgy in Georges May's *Tragédie cornélienne, tragédie racinienne* (Illinois, 1948). In English, Martin Turnell's *The Classical Moment* (New Directions, 1948) includes a section on Corneille. There are two excellent chapters in *Studies in Seventeenth-Century French Literature, presented to Morris Bishop* (Cornell, 1963), and a full-length study by Robert J. Nelson: *Corneille:* His Heroes *and Their Worlds* (Pennsylvania, 1963).